A GOLDEN BOOK • NEW YORK

This 2011 edition published in the United States by Golden Books, an imprint of Random House
Children's Books, a division of Random House, Inc., 1745 Broadway, New York, NY 10019.
Bible Heroes of the Old Testament copyright © 2004 by Random House, Inc.
Bible Stories of Boys and Girls copyright © 2010 by Random House, Inc.
Miracles of Jesus copyright © 2000, 2009 by Random House, Inc.
All rights reserved. Published in the United States by Golden Books, an imprint of Random House
Children's Books, a division of Random House, Inc., 1745 Broadway, New York, NY 10019.
Golden Books, A Golden Book, A Little Golden Book, the G colophon, and the distinctive gold spine
are registered trademarks of Random House, Inc.
www.randomhouse.com/kids
Educators and librarians, for a variety of teaching tools, visit us at
www.randomhouse.com/teachers
Library of Congress Control Number: 2010921824
ISBN: 978-0-375-86523-7
PRINTED IN SINGAPORE
10 9 8 7 6 5 4 3 2 1

BIBLE HEROES

By Christin Ditchfield • Illustrated by Ande Cook

Adam

Adam was the very first person who ever lived. When the world was still brand-new, God brought all the animals he had created to Adam. "Butterfly . . . lion . . . hippopotamus . . . giraffe." There, in the beautiful Garden of Eden, Adam gave every creature a name.

Noah

This is Noah, who obeyed God in a time when other men didn't. One day, God told him there would be a terrible flood to wash away all the wickedness on earth. God told Noah to build a great big boat—called an ark—to save his family and all the animals in the world.

After the animals came to Noah, two by two, it began to rain. Soon the whole world was covered with water, but God kept everyone inside the ark safe and dry. Sometimes Noah's family wondered if it would ever stop raining, but Noah trusted God.

One day, the sun came out, and a beautiful rainbow appeared in the sky. The rainbow was God's promise that there would never be a flood like that again.

Joseph

Once there was a boy named Joseph. His father loved him very much. When Joseph's father gave him a beautiful coat of many colors, Joseph's brothers were jealous. They sold him as a slave, far away in Egypt. But God watched over Joseph as he grew up, because He had a plan for him.

One night, Pharaoh, the king of Egypt, had a frightening dream. With God's help, Joseph told Pharaoh that the dream meant hungry times were coming. Joseph said that the king must start to store up food for his people.

The king was very pleased with Joseph's advice. Years later when the dream came true, Joseph had become king! He'd stored up enough food to feed all the people in the land. Now Joseph understood why God had wanted him to live in Egypt. And he forgave his brothers for what they had done to him.

Miriam

Many years later, God's people were living in Egypt. A new ruler forced them to work as slaves. He even sent his soldiers to harm all the newborn boys. When a baby named Moses was born, his mother laid him in a basket and hid it among the reeds by the riverbank.

Moses' big sister, Miriam, was very brave. Day after day, she stood at the edge of the water, keeping watch over Baby Moses. One day, the king's daughter saw the baby in the basket. She felt sorry for him and took him back to the palace to live with her. And Miriam knew that Moses would be safe.

Moses

When Moses grew up, he led God's people out of Egypt, away from the wicked king. But when the king sent his army to capture them and bring them back, the people were trapped between the soldiers and the Red Sea!

Moses knew that God would help His people. So Moses raised his staff. A mighty wind blew, and the waters parted! When the soldiers tried to follow the people, the water came crashing over them. Moses was the greatest leader his people had ever known.

Joshua

After Moses died, Joshua became the leader of God's people.
God told Joshua to destroy the wicked city of Jericho—but
not with swords or spears. God ordered His people to march
around and around the city walls.

The people wondered how they could possibly win a
battle just by marching. But Joshua trusted God. When
Joshua gave the signal, the people let out a great shout of
praise to God. The earth shook—and the city walls came
tumbling down!

Samson

Samson was the strongest man in the whole world. When his enemies hid in their great walled city, Samson pulled the city gates right off the hinges. God gave Samson the strength to knock down an entire stadium with one giant push!

Deborah

When God's people had problems, they came to Deborah.
Deborah was a very wise woman. She helped the people
to understand and obey God's commands.

One day, when enemies attacked, the people were terrified. The commander of the army refused to lead his soldiers into battle unless Deborah went with them! So Deborah bravely led the way.

David

Once a shepherd boy named David heard a giant named Goliath cursing God and His people. Though he was just a boy, David went out to fight Goliath all by himself.

The giant laughed when he saw David coming. But David had prayed that God would guide his hands. He put a small stone into his slingshot and hurled it toward Goliath. The stone hit the giant right in the middle of his forehead—and he fell at David's feet.

As a shepherd boy, David wrote many beautiful songs of praise to God. After he had killed Goliath, David grew up to be a brave and mighty warrior. He sang songs to thank God for giving him victory over his enemies. God was so pleased with David that He made him king over all the people.

Solomon

In time, David's son Solomon became king. God was pleased that Solomon did not pray for riches, but for an understanding heart. God made King Solomon the wisest man who ever lived, and people came from all over the world to listen to his words. They brought him gifts of gold, silver, and precious jewels. King Solomon used these treasures to build a glorious temple where everyone could worship God.

Elijah

Have you heard of Elijah? He listened closely to God and gave God's messages to others. He taught the way of God in a wicked time. And with God's mighty power, Elijah performed many miracles.

When he had finished the work God gave him to do, Elijah was carried into heaven in a chariot of fire.

Esther

Queen Esther was not only beautiful, but brave. One day, she discovered that a wicked man had come up with a plan to destroy all of God's people.

The law said that no one could talk to the king without permission—not even the queen! But Esther went to the king anyway. Bowing low before his throne, she begged him to protect the people. The king listened to Esther. Because she had the courage to speak up, Queen Esther saved the lives of thousands of people.

Daniel

Daniel was the king's closest friend. He helped the king make important decisions. The king's other friends grew jealous of Daniel, so they set a trap for him.

They tricked the king into making a new law: Anyone who didn't pray to the king would be thrown into a den of fierce, hungry lions. The men knew that Daniel would not pray to the king because Daniel prayed only to God. So when Daniel broke the law, he was thrown into the lions' den!

The next morning, the king rushed to the lions' den to see what had happened. He called out, "Daniel, has your God saved you?"

"It's all right, Your Majesty," called Daniel. "God sent His angel to shut the mouths of the lions." Daniel had trusted God. And God had protected Daniel.

Jonah

Do you know the story of Jonah? God had an important job for him, but Jonah didn't want to do it. So he sailed away on a ship and tried to hide from God. But a terrible storm washed Jonah overboard—and then a big fish swallowed him.

Inside the fish, Jonah felt scared and lonely. "Lord," he prayed, "I'm sorry for running away. Please help me!"

Just then, the fish spat Jonah out onto the shore! This time, Jonah did just what God wanted him to do. He traveled to a city called Nineveh and told the people there how to please God. And God was pleased with Jonah.

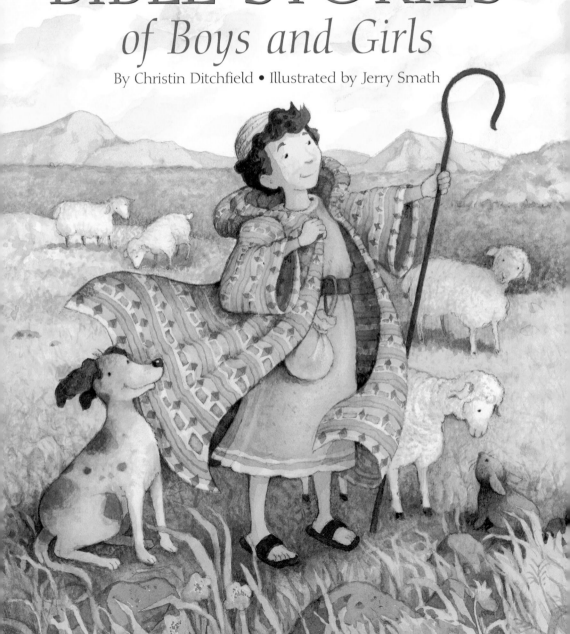

BIBLE STORIES
of Boys and Girls

By Christin Ditchfield • Illustrated by Jerry Smath

The Bible is full of stories of boys and girls who did great things for God. They loved Him with all their hearts and learned to walk in His ways.

REBEKAH THE KINDHEARTED

Every evening, Rebekah joined the other girls
from her village as they went to the well to draw
fresh water for their families. Rebekah had to carry
a large pitcher on her shoulder. When it was full,
it was very heavy.

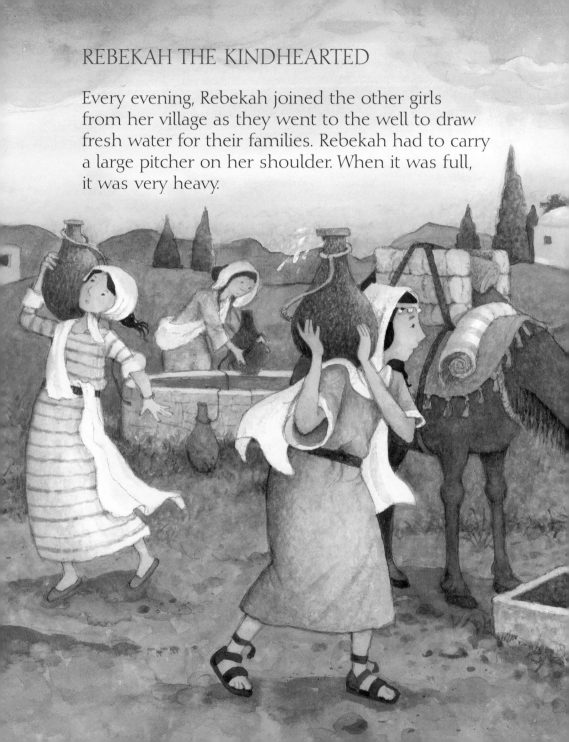

One night, a weary traveler came to the well.
He was hot and thirsty. His camels were thirsty, too!

"Please give me a little water from your jar," the
traveler said to Rebekah.

Rebekah gave water to the man and said, "I'll
draw water for your camels, too." It was hard work,
but Rebekah didn't mind.

The traveler was touched by Rebekah's kindness. He had been praying that God would help him find a very special young woman to marry Isaac, his master's son. The master was Abraham, a great man of God.

Now the traveler knew that God had answered his prayers. He asked Rebekah to introduce him to her family. He gave them gifts of gold and silver and fine jewels, for Rebekah had been chosen by God to marry Isaac.

JOSEPH THE DREAMER

Once there was a boy named Joseph. Joseph's father loved him very much. He gave him a gift of a beautiful coat of many colors. This made Joseph's brothers jealous.

God gave Joseph special dreams about things that would happen in the future. Joseph often dreamed that he would do something very important one day, and that his family would be grateful to him.

Joseph's brothers got tired of hearing him
talk about his dreams. They wanted to get rid of
him, so they sold him as a slave. He was taken
far away to Egypt. But God watched over Joseph
as he grew up in that land, because He had a
very special plan for him.

One night, Pharaoh, the king of Egypt, had a frightening dream. With God's help, Joseph told Pharaoh that the dream meant hungry times were coming. Joseph said that the king must start storing up food for his people so that they would have enough to eat for many years.

The king was very pleased with Joseph. "You shall be in charge of my palace and all my people," he told him.

Years later, when Pharaoh's dream came true, there was enough food stored up to feed all the people in the land, and no one went hungry. Now Joseph understood why God had wanted him to live in Egypt. He forgave his brothers for what they had done to him. He even invited them to come and live with him in Egypt so that he could take care of them and their families. They were very grateful—just as he'd dreamed they would be!

MIRIAM THE GOOD SISTER

Many years later, God's people were still living in Egypt. A new ruler forced them to work as slaves. He even sent soldiers to harm all the newborn Hebrew boys. When a baby named Moses was born, his mother wanted to keep him safe. She laid him in a basket and hid it among the reeds by the riverbank.

Moses's older sister, Miriam, was very brave. Day after day, she stood at the edge of the water, watching over the baby. She prayed that God would protect Moses and keep him hidden from the soldiers.

One day, the king's daughter came to the river to swim and found the basket with the baby in it, crying.

"This is one of the Hebrew babies," said the princess. She felt sorry for Moses and decided to keep him. "But someone must care for him," she said.

Miriam came out from her hiding place. "Shall I bring a Hebrew woman to nurse the baby for you?" she asked.

"Yes, go," answered the princess. So Miriam ran and brought her own mother. The princess told her, "Take this baby and nurse him for me, and I will pay you."

The baby Moses would grow up to lead God's people out of slavery in Egypt and back to their homeland. And his sister, Miriam, would be with him every step of the way.

SAMUEL THE PROPHET

Long ago, a woman named Hannah prayed and prayed that God would give her a son. She promised that if He did, she would give the boy back to Him—she would teach her child to love God and serve Him all his life. God answered Hannah's prayers. He gave her Samuel.

When Samuel was still a little boy, his mother took him to live in the temple. There he would learn to serve God.

One night, Samuel heard a voice calling to him. He thought it was Eli, the priest. But when he ran to Eli's room, Samuel found the priest fast asleep. He hadn't called Samuel.

Three times Samuel heard the voice, and three times he ran to Eli. Finally, Eli realized that Samuel was hearing the voice of God.

"The next time you hear the voice," Eli told Samuel, "say, 'Here I am, Lord. I am listening.'"

That night, God spoke to Samuel. He told
Samuel that He wanted him to be His prophet,
His messenger to the people of Israel. All his
life, Samuel would listen to hear God's voice.
Whenever God spoke to him, Samuel would
tell the people everything that God had said.
He would teach them to listen to God, too.

DAVID THE SHEPHERD KING

David was a shepherd boy. His father had put
him in charge of watching over the family's sheep.
Out in the fields, David learned to play instruments
and write songs of praise to God. When danger did
come, David called on God for help. God gave him
the strength to fight off a lion and a bear to protect
his flock of sheep.

One day, David's father asked him to take some food and supplies to his older brothers, who were soldiers in King Saul's army. When David found his brothers, they were shaking with fear. Their enemies had sent a great giant named Goliath to attack them. It made David angry to hear Goliath cursing God and His people.

"I will fight Goliath myself," said David. The giant laughed when he saw the boy coming. But David prayed that God would guide his hands. He put a small stone into his slingshot and hurled it toward Goliath. The stone hit the giant right in the middle of his forehead— and he fell at David's feet.

David grew up to be a brave and mighty warrior. He led the people of Israel into battle against their enemies time and time again. David always asked God to show him what to do. And God was so pleased with David's courage and faith that He made him king.

JESUS, THE SON OF GOD

Jesus was born in Bethlehem, the same city as David. Like David, He would grow up to be a king—the King of Kings.

Even as a child, Jesus was full of God's wisdom. He understood better than anyone how to live a life that pleased God. One day, His mother, Mary, thought she had lost Him. She looked for the little boy everywhere. At last she found Jesus in the Temple, teaching the priests about God's law.

Jesus wanted to help people everywhere grow closer to God and feel His love for them in their hearts.

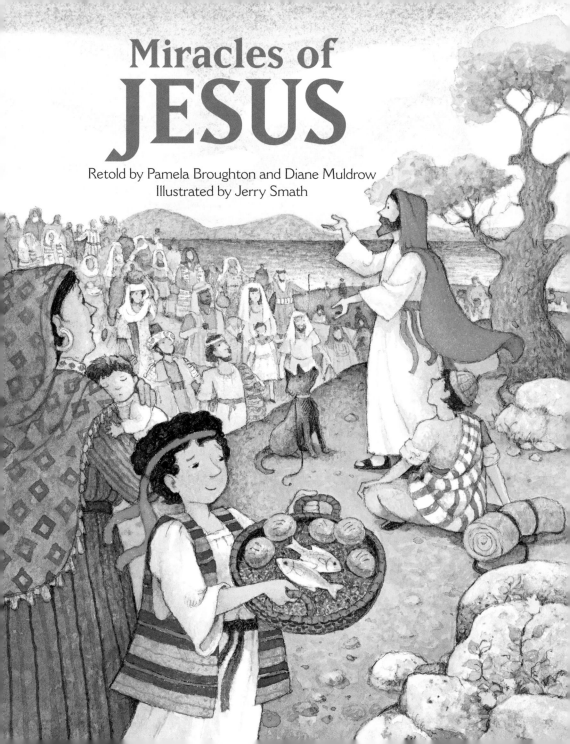

Miracles of
JESUS

Retold by Pamela Broughton and Diane Muldrow
Illustrated by Jerry Smath

One day, after Jesus had begun to teach the gospel of God, He sent His disciples out to teach and heal people far and wide.

When the disciples returned, they wanted to tell Jesus what they had done while they were away. But the town was crowded and noisy.

Jesus said, "Let us go to a quiet place and rest awhile."

So Jesus and the disciples rowed across the Sea of Galilee to a quiet place.

The people saw Jesus leaving. They watched to see where He was heading. Then they took a shorter way to the quiet place.

When Jesus reached the other shore, people were already gathered there.

The people seemed like lost sheep to Jesus. He
knew that they needed Him to be their shepherd.
So He healed those who were sick . . .

. . . and He comforted those who were unhappy.

Then Jesus went up a mountain with His disciples. He looked down and saw that the crowd had grown even larger. There were about five thousand men, and many women and children.

It grew late. Jesus told His disciples, "Give the people something to eat."

The disciple Philip said, "Even two hundred silver coins would not be enough to buy food for all of them."

Jesus said, "How much food is here? Go and see."
The disciple Andrew answered, "There is a boy
with five loaves of barley bread and two small
fishes. But how can we feed so many people
with so little food?"

Jesus took the bread and looked up to Heaven. Then
He blessed the loaves and broke them. He handed the
pieces to His disciples to give to the people.

The fishes, too, were broken and given to the people. And, though it was only a little, and the crowd was huge, there was plenty for everyone after Jesus had blessed the food.

When the people had finished eating, Jesus told His disciples to gather up the leftover pieces of bread and fish.

They filled twelve big baskets with the pieces that were left after everyone had eaten.

The people wondered at the miracle Jesus had worked, feeding five thousand people with only five loaves of bread and two fishes.

At the end of the day, Jesus sent the people home.
He told His disciples to row back across the lake.
Jesus said He would come to them later.

Then Jesus went up the mountain to pray.

That night, a strong wind began to blow. The
disciples were in their boat in the middle of the lake.
Jesus was alone on land.

Jesus saw that the disciples were in serious
trouble, rowing hard and struggling against the wind
and the waves.

In the middle of the night, Jesus went to the men, walking on top of the water.

The men were afraid. They thought Jesus was a ghost. But Jesus spoke to them at once.

"It's all right," He said. "I am here. Don't be afraid!"

Then Jesus climbed into the boat, and the wind stopped.

The disciples were astonished at what they had seen. "Truly, you are the Son of God," they said.

The next morning, Jesus and His disciples arrived
on the other side of the lake and got out of the boat.
The people standing there recognized Jesus at once.
They began carrying sick people to Him on mats.

From then on, in villages and in cities and out on
the farms, people laid the sick before Him.

And all who were touched by Jesus were healed.